W9-BKE-133

Lootas

Lootas
little wave eater

AN ORPHANED SEA OTTER'S STORY

Clare Hodgson Meeker

Photographs by C.J. Casson

SASQUATCH BOOKS
SEATTLE

A Sea Otter Pup Is Born

All alone, in the cold, quiet waters of Uganik Bay in southern Alaska, a sea otter gave birth to a female pup. Floating on her back, the mother licked the small wet ball of fur nestled on her belly. Water glistened on the pup's silvery coat. She had a big snout, elf-like ears, and long, silver whiskers. Slowly, the pup opened her eyes for the first time.

For the next few hours, the mother licked, rubbed, and blew air into the pup's thick fur until it was clean and dry. This careful grooming trapped millions of tiny air bubbles in the fur and kept the cold water away from the baby otter's skin.

When she was finished, the mother placed the little pup in the water next to her while she groomed herself. Fluffed up and dry, the pup floated like a cork on the glassy surface. But as soon

A mother sea otter nuzzles her pup shortly after its birth.

as the mother heard the pup's soft, whistling cries, she scooped her back up onto her belly to nurse on mother's milk.

The only time the mother left her pup alone was when she had to dive for food. Before she dove, she wrapped the pup in floating kelp for protection. The thick, rubbery strands hid the helpless pup from sharp-eyed eagles and anchored her from strong ocean currents that might carry her away.

The mother returned a few minutes later with a sea urchin tucked under her arm. The little pup watched her mother bite through the quilled outer shell with her crushing teeth and suck out the insides.

Sea Kelp and food

Where there are sea otters, there is sure to be sea kelp. Otters use kelp—the fastest-growing plant species in the world—to hide their pups and to find tasty sea urchins, which thrive among kelp beds. Sea otters also eat squid, crab, clams, and other shellfish.

Then it was time for the pup to nurse again. Safely wrapped in her mother's warm paws, the little sea otter soon fell asleep.

Within a week, the pup began to practice swimming, to prepare for life at sea. Using her mother as a launching pad, she paddled and splashed in the water on her stomach for several minutes at a time. Sometimes, when the wind blew and the water grew choppy, the mother swam underneath the tired pup and lifted her up with her back.

Within a month, the pup was grooming her own tail and flippers. Like a budding acrobat, she licked and blew air into her fur while riding on her mother's belly. But she could not yet feed or groom herself completely. She would still need her mother's care for a few months more.

Insulation

With half a million hairs per square inch, otters have the densest fur of any mammal—which helps them stay warm in their cold ocean home. Constant grooming traps air bubbles next to the skin to prevent water from penetrating. When a sea otter dives, the air bubbles escape and must be carefully restored by the otter fluffing and blowing its fur.

Orphaned ...But Not Alone

All fluffed up after a thorough grooming.

Summertime brought warmer weather, but also new danger. The once quiet bay now hummed with the loud sound of motorboats from the fish cannery on the rocky shore. Farther out in the bay, a group of sea otters linked paws and rafted together for safety. But the mother and her pup stayed in the shallower water where it was easier to find food.

Early one gray morning, a thick mist covered the water, muffling all sound. The mother floated peacefully with her pup, as gentle waves danced around them. Suddenly, the stuttering pitch of a motorboat burst through the silence. Sitting straight up in the water, the mother looked to see where the noise was coming from. The sound of breaking waves and whining engine grew close and loud. With no time

Lootas' rescue

"The frightened pup hissed as the woman lifted her into the boat."

to dive, the mother grabbed the pup and rolled over.

There was a loud thump as the boat struck, and the pup felt her mother's body pulled away. Struggling alone in the choppy water, the little sea otter cried out for her mother in shrill, piercing screams.

A young woman in the boat looked back to see a small sea otter bobbing up and down in the waves.

"We must have hit and killed that pup's mother," the woman yelled to the driver. "We have to save it."

"But we can't just pick up a sea otter pup," said the driver. "It's against the law."

"What if it is injured?" cried the woman. "Those screams will haunt me if we don't do something now." So the boat turned around.

The frightened pup hissed as the woman

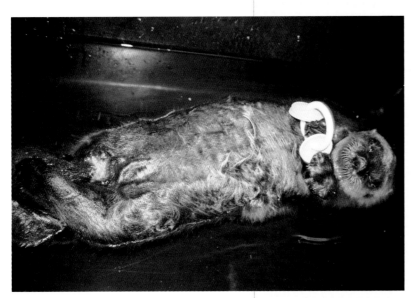

After her wounds are treated, the injured pup rests quietly.

lifted her into the boat. The woman held the little sea otter on her lap and gently rubbed her back with a towel. Slowly, the pup calmed down.

"She is hurt," said the woman, noticing a gash on the pup's left flipper. "We need to get her to a veterinarian right away." The boat sped back to the cannery where the woman phoned the local wildlife authorities.

With help from a park ranger and a Kodiak veterinarian, the injured pup was put on a plane later that day bound for Anchorage, Alaska. There she was taken to the U.S. Fish and Wildlife Service, which cares for stranded sea otter pups.

The pup's eyes opened wide under the bright lights as biologist Carol Gorbics and a marine mammal veterinarian examined her injuries. She had a slight fever, an injured flipper, and cuts

Carol Gorbics gently holds the baby sea otter.

Exhausted, the little pup peacefully sleeps.

When she wakes, she checks out her new surroundings.

that needed stitches. But considering all that she had been through, the pup was surprisingly strong.

It was now up to Carol to decide what to do with her. A sea otter pup belongs in the wild. But the one-month-old pup was too young to survive there without her mother.

Her best chance for life was under a trained human's care. But who would be willing to devote the time and money it would take to hand-raise an orphaned pup?

Just then, the pup gave out a soft, whistling cry. Carol gently picked her up. Comforted by the warmth of her touch, the little sea otter rested quietly in Carol's arms.

"You are one brave pup," said Carol, smiling at her. "We will name you Lootas, the Wave Eater, in honor of your Alaskan home. But now, Lootas, we must find you a new home."

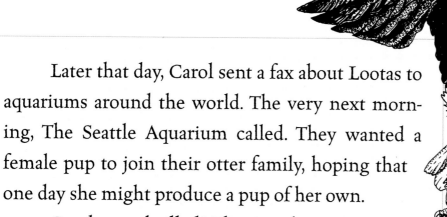

Later that day, Carol sent a fax about Lootas to aquariums around the world. The very next morning, The Seattle Aquarium called. They wanted a female pup to join their otter family, hoping that one day she might produce a pup of her own.

Carol was thrilled! The Seattle Aquarium had an award-winning sea otter program directed by marine biologist C.J. Casson. A tall, easy-going man with a quick sense of humor, C.J. had the right temperament for this difficult job. He and his staff had bred and raised sea otters before, but this would be the first time they would hand-raise a pup themselves. The aquarium offered to fly Lootas to Seattle the next week.

"Orphaned but not alone" read the *Anchorage Daily News* headline as news of Lootas' rescue quickly spread. Meanwhile, Carol and her staff worked around the clock to prepare Lootas for her new life. Every four hours, they bathed, groomed,

Predators

Sea otters, which can weigh up to 100 pounds or more, have few enemies and are near the top of the coastal food chain. Their predators include sharks, orcas, eagles, bears, and humans.

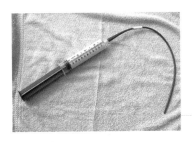

Lootas' feeding tube.

Peek-a-boo!

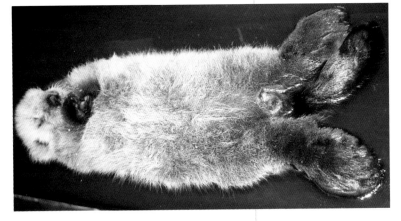

Dreaming comes easy for
a sea otter pup.

and tried to feed her. But the transition from a mother otter's care to human care was not easy.

The shock of injury and loss had finally settled in. Having nursed only on her mother's milk, Lootas would not take liquid from a bottle. Knowing she could die if she became dehydrated, Carol's staff had to insert a straw-size tube down Lootas' throat to feed her.

Lootas often woke up crying. The staff wanted to hold the pup to comfort her, but they knew that a wild animal cannot be handled like a household pet. Besides, Lootas still had a fever. If she was held too much, her body temperature could rise to a dangerous level. So instead, Lootas was given cool baths to relax her.

From Anchorage to Seattle

By the end of the week, Lootas was doing better. She had started to nurse from a bottle while she slept, and her flipper had begun to heal.

The Seattle Aquarium arranged for an infant-animal-care specialist from Seattle's Woodland Park Zoo to accompany Lootas to Seattle. The day of the flight, Carol tucked Lootas into her traveling bed—a blue plastic laundry basket packed with ice and covered with nylon netting. "I wish you didn't have to leave Alaska," said Carol, rubbing the little pup's flipper one last time. "But you will teach the world a lot about sea otters." She then closed the netting over Lootas' bed for the journey to her new home.

In Seattle, C.J. waited at the airport for Lootas'

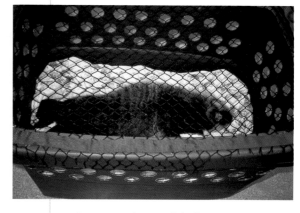

Lootas arrives safely in Seattle in her travel bed.

Aquarium entrance on Seattle's waterfront.

Otter tubs.

A makeshift otter nursery in the aquarium basement.

Lootas floats in her play tub.

plane to arrive. As he watched the blue plastic tub being unloaded, he wondered how Lootas had survived the long flight. He peeked through the netting, not knowing what to expect.

Lootas stared back at him, wide-eyed and curious. "Eek, eek," she cried in a high-pitched greeting. She was propped like a queen on her throne of ice.

Lootas continued to scream the whole way home. When they arrived at the aquarium, Lootas was carried down to the basement nursery and placed in the crib-size waterbed the staff had built for her. But having slept for most of the flight, Lootas was in no mood to nap.

The nursery also contained two small plastic tubs filled with cold sea water: one for Lootas to use as a toilet and the other for her to play in. C.J. put Lootas into the toilet tub first and then quickly lifted her out so she would not soil her fur.

Then he put Lootas in the second tub so she could play. The salty water helped to clean her fur. But after paddling on her stomach for a few minutes, Lootas again began to scream.

"I may have to invest in ear plugs," said C.J., lifting Lootas onto his lap. Grabbing a towel off the top of a stack, he began to dry her fur. Lootas stopped crying and started to help him, rubbing her face with her paws.

C.J. finished drying the baby otter's fur with a cool-air hair dryer. But Lootas would not keep still.

Coastline

Lootas journeyed from the icy waters off Alaska's Kodiak Island to her new home in Seattle, Washington. Kodiak was one of the few remaining homes for the northern sea otter at the turn of the century. They now live in waters as far south as Washington State.

ALASKA

Anchorage

Kodiak

Juneau

BRITISH COLUMBIA

Vancouver

Seattle

WASHINGTON

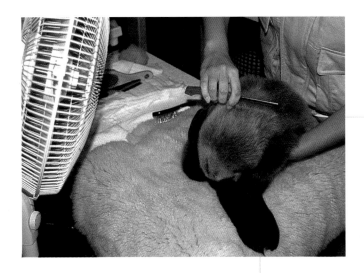

The grooming process (clockwise from top): After towel-drying, a cool-air fan is used to finish drying the fur; brushing removes tangles; a fine-toothed comb reaches every hair; fluffed up and dry, Lootas relaxes on C.J.'s shoulder.

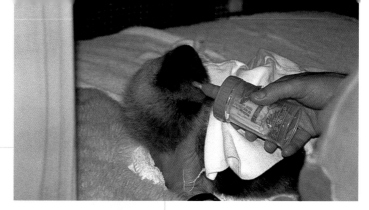

Top to bottom: Lootas
would take a bottle only
when she was sleeping;
plastic keys were a
favorite chew toy;
Lootas uses her chest as
a table for playing and
eating; so many toys, so
little time . . .

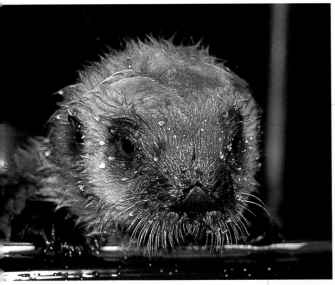

No time to dry off—gotta go!

Lootas is quickly removed from the toilet tub so she won't soil her fur.

"You are so busy to go somewhere," he said, wrestling to hold onto Lootas and the hair dryer too. In the wild, sea otters are constantly moving to stay clean and warm in the cold water.

Once her fur was dry, it still had to be untangled and fluffed up using a fine-toothed comb. With half a million hairs per square inch, Lootas' coat took a whole hour to groom.

After three hours of bathing and grooming, Lootas was put back in the waterbed. While the gentle wave motion rocked her to sleep, C.J. prepared formula for her bottle, including a warm mixture of finely chopped clam and squid, whipping cream, cod liver oil, and vitamins.

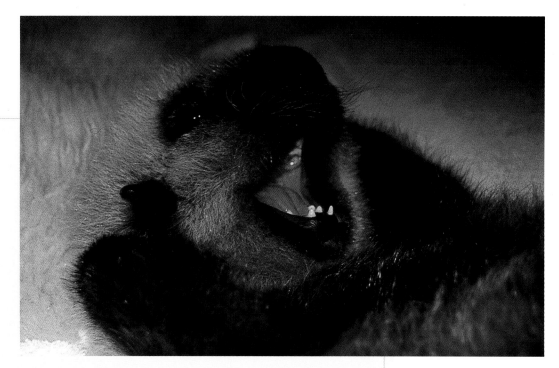

Break time for Lootas.

Lootas drank the warm liquid while she slept. Finally, C.J. could sit down to relax. If he was lucky, she would sleep for two hours before he had to bathe and groom her again. This routine would be repeated five times a day for at least another month, until Lootas could groom herself.

But in that quiet moment, C.J. looked down at the pup and smiled. "It's a good thing you're so cute," he whispered, "because you're one high-maintenance kid."

A final touch-up before nap time.

A little ocean motion on the
waterbed calms Lootas down.

Time to Play

for four straight days, C.J. cared for Lootas day and night. It was better for her to get used to one person first, before introducing the rest of his team of care-givers. Still fevered and not eating much, Lootas was not out of danger yet.

Confused by her surroundings, Lootas screamed much of the time. At first, C.J. tried to respond to each cry. Was she hungry, was she bored, or did she just miss her mother? Even when he tried to rest, her

Lootas falls asleep with comb in paw.

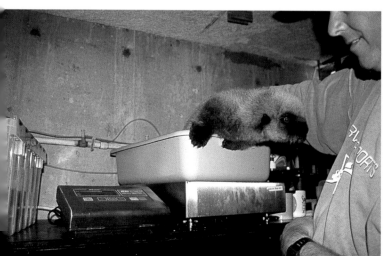

Lootas enjoys her morning weigh-in.

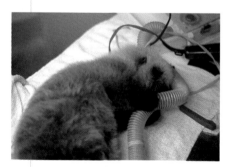

Asleep in the middle of things again!

19

C.J. gives Lootas her own guided tour of the aquarium.

shrill cries haunted his sleep.

By the end of the week, C.J. was exhausted. So he called in his four-person team to share twelve-hour shifts so that he could go home and sleep.

Shucking mussels for Lootas.

Once C.J. was rested and thinking clearly again, he realized it was better not to respond to Lootas' every cry. If they waited a bit, sometimes Lootas solved her own problems.

One morning, Lootas was having a hard time sleeping. Only a curtain separated her nursery from the busy, behind-the-scenes activity of the aquarium staff. As one member of the team stood beside Lootas' bed talking, Lootas looked up at her and gave a short, high shriek. The woman lowered her voice, but

Lootas chews on a mussel.

Lootas takes a mussel from a member of the team.

Lootas continued to stare at her and shriek until the woman was finally silent.

Lootas was able to sleep better once she started to eat solid food. Within two weeks of her arrival at the aquarium, she gobbled up twenty-five mussels at a feeding. Like sea otter pups in the wild, Lootas needed to eat a third of her body weight each day to stay healthy.

At two months old, Lootas weighed eight pounds. C.J. was pleased. "At my weight, I'd have to eat two hundred Big Macs a day to keep up with you," he teased.

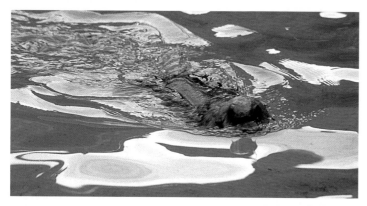

Once Lootas started to swim, C.J. had to struggle to keep up with her in his heavy rubber waders.

23

Lootas tries to climb out of her plastic pool.

A member of the team offers Lootas a clam.

As Lootas grew stronger, she began to spend more time in the water. She now played in the plastic nursery pool as much as she rested. She kept her favorite toy, a yellow ducky rattle, tucked under her arm, when she wasn't chewing on it. And she loved to drag a wash cloth around the pool as if it were kelp.

C.J. and the team made other toys to keep Lootas busy. They froze small blocks of ice with a mussel or crab leg inside for her to eat.

Much more active and curious now, Lootas tried to climb out of her plastic pool the way an otter in the wild would climb out onto a rock. But without a ledge, she could fall and hurt herself. It was time to move Lootas to a larger outdoor pool.

A dishpan makes an excellent boat for a baby sea otter!

Lootas' coat darkens as she loses her baby fur.

Every day, the team took turns keeping Lootas company in the cold outdoor pool. At first, Lootas insisted on holding someone's hand while she floated on her back. But once she got used to the larger space, she raced back and forth across the length of the pool while the team members struggled to keep up with her in their heavy rubber waders.

One day, Lootas tried to dive. For an otter, learning to dive is as important as a bird learning to fly. Again and again, she dipped her head into the water. But her woolly coat would not let her sink.

This soon changed, however. By the end of her third month of life, Lootas had shed her woolly coat. Her fur was now a smoky brown and as sleek and soft as feathers.

Once she could dive, Lootas discovered a whole new underwater world. Sea otters are very intelligent beings and one of the few mammals to use tools to get food. At mealtime, C.J. tossed clams into the water for Lootas to catch. With eyes open, she dove under the water and snatched up the clams in her paws. Popping back up to the surface, she floated on her back and knocked the two clams together to open them.

In the wild, sea otters spend all their time trying to stay alive. But Lootas had plenty of time to get into mischief. One day, when the pool wasn't draining

Paw-fect

A skeletal view of the sea otter's forepaw shows five digits, like a human's fingers. Thickly padded, these paws can safely hold a spiky sea urchin or grip a stone. The short, powerful arms are perfect for hammering open shellfish.

right, C.J. discovered that the drain pipe was blocked with bits of clam shell. Another time, missing one of Lootas' feeding bowls, he found her playing with it at the bottom of the pool.

Lootas steals a plastic bench, as the mischief continues.

First Meeting

By late September, Lootas was four months old. C.J. was proud of how well she had adapted to her new life at the aquarium. Lootas weighed over fourteen pounds and ate fifty mussels at a feeding. She also groomed herself on her own, rolling and twirling in the cold salt water, scrubbing under her arms and blowing into her fur. Clearly at home in the water now, she no longer needed twenty-four-hour care. Everyone looked forward to getting back to a normal schedule.

But Lootas still had not met the other sea otters in the aquarium. C.J. decided that she should meet the female

Fortified by food, so . . .

. . . bring on the other otters!

29

As sea otters age, their fur turns white or gray, as on Etika.

Kenai sniffs Lootas' cage: Where is all that noise coming from?

otters first. Perhaps one of them would adopt Lootas as her pup.

Etika, the grandmother of the aquarium's otter family, was twenty-seven years old. She was also the world's oldest sea otter living in an aquarium. She had given birth to four pups and raised them herself. But now Etika was deaf and blind.

When Lootas and Etika met, Lootas tumbled and rolled playfully around her, as if trying to get her attention. But Etika ignored her. She had neither the interest nor the energy to keep up with a young pup.

Kenai, the other female, was the right age to be a mother to Lootas. Kenai was orphaned by the Exxon Valdez oil spill, when an oil tanker ran aground in Prince William Sound killing several thousand sea otters. Raised at the Point Defiance Zoo & Aquarium in nearby Tacoma, Kenai came to The Seattle Aquarium as an eight-year-old adult.

Lootas and Kenai check each other out.

Things started off well between Kenai and Lootas. Lootas swam over and sniffed Kenai. Kenai dove under-water and Lootas followed, curious to see what she was up to. But at mealtime, Kenai stole Lootas' food and Lootas backed off, afraid.

C.J. wished that Kenai and Lootas had gotten along better in their first meeting, but at least they hadn't fought. The next step was to introduce Lootas to the main sea otter pool, which would

Lootas clings to the boot of her human friend.

be her permanent home. Since the pool was four times as deep as the one she was used to, C.J. decided that Lootas should try it out without the other otters first.

The following Sunday morning, a small group of staff and volunteers gathered for the special event. Pulling on a wet suit, flippers, hood, and gloves, C.J. jumped into the pool to keep Lootas company. But Lootas seemed quite comfortable, bounding into the pool and disappearing underwater.

"Well, I guess I'm not needed here," said C.J., addressing the crowd. Lootas had hauled herself out of the water and was sitting on the concrete deck alone.

Underwater Roll

Propelled by rear flippers shaped like paddles, the sea otter moves gracefully through the water. Rolling and twirling is not just for fun, it is also an important part of grooming. The otter's flexible spine helps it to clean every inch of its fur.

Suddenly, she whipped her head from side to side and let out a shrill, piercing scream. Diving into the water, Lootas raced over to C.J. and climbed wildly all over him. But with the rubber clothing covering him from head to foot, she did not recognize him.

Seeing her panic, C.J. tore off his hood and gloves and wrapped his arms around the frightened pup. "It's okay, it's okay," he said in a soothing tone as he swam with her to the side of the pool.

It took the whole day to calm Lootas down. But eventually, she fell asleep in the main otter pool and slept there through the night.

Humans must wear a special diving suit to keep warm in cold water. Lootas wants to help keep the diver warm, too!

C.J. stayed up late that night, worrying about Lootas. His plans for her future were suddenly in doubt. Lootas needed to learn to behave like a sea

Relatives

The sea otter, or *Enhydra lutris* (its genus and species name), first came to inhabit the north Pacific Ocean roughly three million years ago. Larger and heavier than its nearest relative, the river otter, the sea otter is a member of a carnivorous mammal family called Mustelidae, which also includes skunks, weasels, and badgers.

otter. But how would she learn, if the other sea otters would not help her?

Thinking back to his childhood home next to the water, C.J. remembered listening to the river otters at night, splashing and chittering to one another. But whenever they saw a human, they quickly swam away.

Like the river otters, Lootas, too, was a wild animal. But having been rescued and raised by humans, she would never be afraid of them. There would always be a special bond between C.J. and Lootas, but it was time for her to join her own otter family.

They had all worked hard to get to this point. He would not give up.

Before entering the main otter pool (clockwise from above): A volunteer spends a quiet moment with Lootas; Lootas is fed; finally, she is ready to take the plunge.

Lootas Finds a Family

Lootas starts a game of hide-and-seek with Kenai.

You're it!

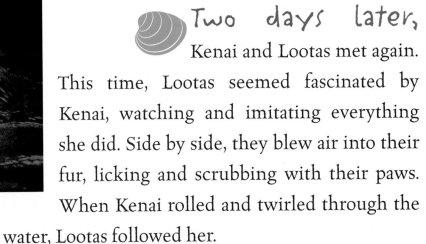 **Two days later,** Kenai and Lootas met again. This time, Lootas seemed fascinated by Kenai, watching and imitating everything she did. Side by side, they blew air into their fur, licking and scrubbing with their paws. When Kenai rolled and twirled through the water, Lootas followed her.

Soon, they began to chase one another, first nipping then darting away. C.J. watched cautiously for any aggressive behavior. But Kenai and Lootas seemed to enjoy each other.

Finally they rested, floating on their backs with paws folded under their chins. With eyes closed, they used their tails as rudders to steer into one another and then drift apart.

Lootas and Kenai meet again

"Lootas seemed fascinated by Kenai, watching
and imitating everything she did."

Within a few days, Kenai's mothering instinct had clearly taken over. She shared her food with Lootas. And whenever one of the team entered the pool area, Kenai grabbed Lootas to keep her away from them.

"It looks like Kenai has adopted Lootas as her pup," said C.J. to his team. "Our parenting job is coming to an end." But they were all going to miss caring for her themselves.

While Kenai and Lootas got to know each other, Kodiak, the male otter in the group, was content to be with his old friend Etika. But in late November, Etika died, and Kodiak was soon lonely. The time had come for him and Lootas to meet.

Male otters in the wild can be very aggressive with females. A sea otter pup the size of Lootas could be killed in one ferocious bite. But C.J.

When a human approaches, Kenai protects Lootas.

wasn't too worried because Kodiak had always been a pretty mellow guy. He, too, was a survivor of the Exxon Valdez oil spill and had been living in aquariums ever since.

Kodiak, the male otter, keeps his distance.

As soon as Kodiak entered the main otter pool, his calm nature was put to the test. Lootas boldly swam up, gave him a few playful nips, and scurried away. But when Kodiak took up the chase, Kenai stopped him with a swift bite. Kodiak decided to keep his distance from the otter pup for the moment.

In December, Lootas was six months old. Very independent now, she had reached the stage where, if in the wild, she and her mother would soon separate.

Kenai keeps a watchful
eye on Lootas . . .

. . . while Lootas just kicks
back and relaxes.

A normal day in
the otter pool.

Today, Lootas lives together with Kenai and Kodiak in the main otter pool. Never shy with people, she is the first to swim up and greet aquarium visitors. Whenever C.J. or a member of the team comes to feed them, Kenai still acts protective. But Lootas always finds a way to escape from Kenai and swim over to be near her old friends.

As the three sea otters swoop and dive together and tend to their daily grooming, it is clear that the little Wave Eater finally belongs to her own otter family.

Lootas (at left) floats happily with her new otter family, Kenai and Kodiak.

Otter love: Perhaps Lootas will become a mother herself someday.

Acknowledgments

The return of the sea otter from near extinction 100 years ago is one of the conservation success stories of this century. Thanks in part to governments and organizations worldwide that united together to ban the hunting of sea otters and to protect their habitat, there are now more than 100,000 sea otters alive today. In the United States, it is against the law to pick up a sea otter pup. Rescuing wild animals requires specialized care by trained experts. Such a rescue effort can end up involving hundreds of trained staff and volunteers. This was especially true in the case of Lootas. We would like to thank the following people, who each played a critical role in Lootas' survival:

In Kodiak, Alaska: Ada Berry, April Mathers, and Jonathan Schafler.

In Anchorage, Alaska: Lysi Bushey, Amy Christiansen, Linda Comerci, Angie Doroff, Kathy Gardner, Carole Gorbics, Tony Fischbach, Gina Hollomon, and Pam Tuomi.

In Seattle, Washington: Thanks to the original otter team of Harmony Frazier, Dr. Janis Ott Joslin, Laura Wymore, Richard Ramsby, Shawn Larson, Angela Smith, and all the volunteers who gave so much to this project. Additional thanks to Robert Anderson, Roland Anderson, Gary Ballew, Jill Bodner, Ken Bounds, Carol Bufi, Mitzi Butler, Mary Carlson, Tim Carpenter, Jeff Christiansen, Dr. Darin Collins, Scott Gaudette, Galen Motin Goff, Marcia Kamin, Bob Kiel, Pat MacMahon, Andrew Mannery, Marty Morris, Sal Muoz, Lora Murphy, Rodger Ogren, Carmen Olds, Ted Parker, S.J. Rajamaran, Bill Robertson, Terry Roche, Susan Schulz, Cindi Shiota, Linda Shipe, Sue Donhue Smith, Robert Stowers, Dale Styers, Marla Tieken, Alan Tomita, Voronica Whitney-Robinson, and The Seattle Aquarium Society.

In Monterey, California: Julie Hymer.

Special thanks to the U.S. Fish and Wildlife Service, The Seattle Aquarium, Woodland Park Zoo, Point Defiance Zoo & Aquarium, and Monterey Bay Aquarium for their educational work and expertise. Understanding sea otter behavior helps us learn how to better protect them as part of the web of life on which our own existence depends.

The Seattle Aquarium was the first aquarium in the world to successfully breed sea otters. Born in the spring of 1979, Tickuk became the first of four sea otters conceived and raised to adulthood. To date, The Seattle Aquarium remains the only institution in the United States with this accomplishment. Successful breeding programs are important because they increase our knowledge of a species, while helping ensure genetic compatibility and diversity among captive populations. A portion of the proceeds from this book will benefit Lootas and The Seattle Aquarium's sea otter breeding program.

Additional sources: *The World of the Sea Otter*, by Stefani Paine and photographs by Jeff Foot (Sierra Club Books, 1993); and *Sea Otters*, by John A. Love (Fulcrum Publishing, 1992).

To Sarah, Sam, and Meredith, my research companions;
to Dan, for his computer skills and patience; and to Kate, my editor,
whose creative vision helped make this book possible. —C.H.M.

For all of the volunteers who helped raise Lootas, your commitment and
dedication are what make the aquarium a success. For Teresa, Karah, and Erin, thanks
for your patience and understanding. So much fur, so little time . . . —C.J.C.

Copyright ©1999 by Clare Hodgson Meeker
Photographs ©1999 by The Seattle Aquarium
All rights reserved. No portion of this book may be reproduced or utilized in any form, or by any electronic,
mechanical, or other means without the prior written permission of the publisher.
Printed in Hong Kong
Distributed in Canada by Raincoast Books, Ltd.
03 02 01   5 4
Cover and interior design: Kate Basart
Large cover photograph: ©Art Wolfe
Interior illustrations: Cooper Illustration
Photographs: Pages 4, 6, 7, 8, and 10 (middle, bottom) by Gina Hollomon;
pages 14, 20, and 23 by Teresa Casson; and page 7 by Connie Barclay, U. S. Fish and Wildlife Service.
All other photographs by C.J. Casson.
Library of Congress Cataloging in Publication Data
Meeker, Clare Hodgson.
Lootas, little wave eater : an orphaned sea otter's story / by Clare Hodgson Meeker ; photographs by C.J. Casson.
Summary: Describes how a young sea otter pup is rescued after its mother
is accidentally killed and finds a new home in the Seattle Aquarium.
ISBN 1-57061-164-5
1. Sea otter—Washington (State)—Seattle—Biography Juvenile literature.
[1. Sea otter. 2. Wildlife rescue. 3. Seattle Aquarium.] I. Casson, C.J., ill. II. Title.
QL737.C25M368 1999
599.769'5'0929—dc21
[B]   99-24722

SASQUATCH BOOKS
615 Second Avenue
Seattle, Washington 98104
(206) 467-4300
books@SasquatchBooks.com
www.SasquatchBooks.com